5 STEPS TO BECOMING A HAPPIER STEPMOM

5 STEPS TO BECOMING A HAPPIER STEPMOM

The Bonus Mommy

DESIREE STEWART

D Stewart, LLC

CONTENTS

Dedication vi

1. STEP 1 - IDENTIFY YOUR STRESSORS 1
2. STEP 2 - BOUNDARIES 9
3. STEP - 3 ASK FOR HELP 14
4. STEP 4 - SELF CARE 18
5. STEP 5- CONFIDENCE 21

About The Author 23

Dedicated to Bae!
Without you, none of this
would be possible!

Thank you for making
my dreams come true!

Copyright © 2021 by D Stewart

All rights reserved. No part of this book may be reproduced in any manner whatsoever without written permission except in the case of brief quotations embodied in critical articles and reviews.

First Printing, 2021

CHAPTER 1

STEP 1 - IDENTIFY YOUR STRESSORS

"STRESS IS THE TRASH OF MODERN LIFE; WE ALL GENERATE IT, BUT IF YOU DON'T DISPOSE OF IT PROPERLY, IT WILL PILE UP AND OVERTAKE YOUR LIFE" - DANZAE PACE

When you recognize what you can and can't control and only focus on fixing what you can! That my friend is FREEDOM!

ARE YOU STRESSED?

It's okay not to be okay.

You might be thinking, "Okay, I'm supporting my husband with his struggles. I'm learning how to be a bonus mom and a wife, but what if I'm not okay? I want to punch this bitch in the face every time I hear of how shitty she is. Sometimes just hearing her name sets me off. How do I move through this situation with grace and humility? How do I keep myself from going off every time she hurts my husband or stepchild?

The role of bonus mom isn't always easy. If you are struggling with your position, let's address it.

1. It's OK to feel like you might lose it. Trust me, honey, you are human, which is a normal feeling. The first step is to be OK because you don't feel OK.
2. In my experience, you will feel guilt wherever you are in your stepmom journey. It's prevalent. Early on in my bonus mom journey, I would feel guilty when my stepdaughter wasn't with us. We did something exciting or memorable. I would feel guilty during routine activities, like family night or eating take-out. There were also phases in my journey where I didn't want to be a bonus mom or deal with the drama, and I would feel guilt for wanting to run away. Whatever you're feeling guilty about, it's ok.

Sometimes things are just crappy, and everything feels heavy. You feel the weight of the world on your shoulders. Once you recognize that, it's ok to feel that way. Sis, put your big girl panties on, get up, and <INSERT SELF CARE>!

STRESSOR #1 - Coparenting

Parenting is already hard enough; throw in another person or two that you'll be parenting with, and it becomes more challenging. I'm not saying you can't have great relationships with each other, but they do have to commit to doing better for their kid(s). Even the best of co-parenting relationships take work. From sharing schedules, kids, and holidays as a stepmom, it often feels like your opinion doesn't matter or that you don't have control over your life or schedule. I get it, and sometimes it just sucks. If both parties want to do the work, you can create a mutually beneficial relationship.

STRESSOR #2 -Adjusting to your new role

Adjusting your new role as a bonus mom isn't an easy one. You might feel like there is no place for you for a while. How your role works also depends on your parenting plan and how involved their mom is in their lives. Suppose your husband's ex is a wonderful mom who doesn't cause drama and wants her kids to be happy; congratulations! Some stepmom isn't as lucky, and your situation is different. Maybe your stepchild's mom is abusive and absent from their life, then your involvement and role as a mother will be needed. I believe once you've decided to be with your spouse, you've also decided to commit to his kids. The kids and the man are a package deal.

I felt like I didn't have a role in my stepdaughter's life. It was a feeling that would come and go throughout the years. She already had a mom and a dad, and then there was me. I have always known I wanted and could give my stepdaughter more than her biological mom could, but I also felt like I was somehow erasing or replacing her mother if I did that. So my solution at the time was to show up for my stepdaughter the best I knew how and before I knew it, I became her go-to person. I became her stability, and I provided her with the home and life I had always wanted her to have.

Adjusting looks different for everyone; some women often change while others may not or take months to change. The goal isn't to compare ourselves or put ourselves on some unreleased timeline. It is to say, hey, we see you; we know how you feel because we have been there before. Just remember it's okay. You are enough, and you are doing enough.

STRESSOR #3 -Schedules and Holidays

Are you dreading every upcoming holiday? Does it give you the anxiety to celebrate without your stepchildren? You are not alone. Many stepmoms say schedules and holidays are the most challenging part of being a stepparent. You have to share the child, so someone isn't going to be happy about the plan. You do not want to do these three things when it comes to holiday schedules.

Don't take it personally - If there is a holiday that isn't your usual holiday and he asks his ex to switch days, she says no. It's ok, don't take it personally. Maybe she had something planned for the child during her time, and she isn't willing to adjust her plan. That is ok, just like it would be if you had planned on a day his ex wants to switch you.

Avoid having unrealistic expectations. There will be many times when you don't like the outcome of a holiday schedule. Still, the best way to deal with this is not to have expectations for the holidays you do get with your stepchild.

Don't compete with his EX. Have you ever found yourself

wanting to make sure your stepchildren have a better holiday <insert any event> with you or at your house? DO NOT COMPETE With his ex! It's not worth it because it'll only make you feel bad.

The Best thing you can do is stay on your side of the street and worry about the things you can control. You can't manage the schedule or exactly how the holiday events will go. Still, you can worry about yourself and the things that go on in your household. Focus on the time you do get with your stepchildren and spouse. After all, it doesn't last forever!

STRESSOR #4 -Dealing with a high conflict EX

Is your spouse's ex-high conflict? Does it feel like no matter what you do, there is always drama and angst when dealing with his ex? Or maybe you don't deal with her at all. High conflict Ex's are exhausting, and it's often tough to reason with them so you can co-parent. The best advice I can give you is this. This up now because you'll need to hear this loud and clear. You can't rationalize with someone that is miserable and wants to argue. Some EX's are holding on to issues from their marriage with your husband. I've seen it with many of my clients where the husband's EX brings drama and conflict because she wants to bring chaos to your life. It could be something as simple as she doesn't like you. The reality is we don't get to tell her how to feel and if her high conflict drama is because she's hurt, you won't be able to get her to understand anything else. So the best way to deal with this is to RESPOND DON'T REACT! I'll repeat that RESPOND DON'T REACT if you find yourself in an argument with his high conflict ex. She is working hard to upset you and get you to engage in her argument. The first thing you do is take three deep breaths. And as for yourself, how do I want to respond to this. Think about ways to respond to the issue but not fly off the deep end by reacting.

A Recommended example of this would be you guys wanted to pick up your stepchild an extra day after school, and his ex agrees to it when he asks. Then he exchanges her mind and creates drama and havoc to make it hard on you guys or make the extra time you requested miserable. If you react with the first thing that comes to mind, you'll react and play right into what she wants you to do. She is unhappy or angry about something, and she can't stand to see you living your best life, so she wants to make it miserable for you. But not today, boo.

Does your husband's high conflict ex manipulate your stepchild to believe things that aren't true about you or your husband?

If a child has an abusive parent, they'll often believe that parents lie because it's the abuse cycle. Some mothers will manipulate their children to think their other parent is evil, abusive, and terrible even if they aren't true. It can cause a child to think that their Mom can do no wrong and anything anyone else says is untrue because they've been groomed to believe this. For example, if his ex gives the child a false or negative narrative about you or your husband.

In a child's eyes, their mom can do no wrong. It can apply

to dads too, but we are just talking about moms for now. Children trust their parents. When a mom puts false information in a child's head, the child might not suspect it because they can't fathom their mother or parent would lie to them. See, as a stepmom, you are a "real" mom. Still, no matter how much you wish you could, you can't replace their biological mom. That is fucking amazing! As adults, we learn coping mechanisms and build up walls to protect ourselves from this scary world. Still, children can love and forgive their absent parents. It doesn't matter that you wipe their tears every time they're hurt, mom is still queen, and it's okay if that bugs you. When your stepchild has an absent, abusive parent, we, as bonus moms, can't help but want to make all the pain go away, but often we can't. You will find yourself in the middle of battles far more extensive than you could ever have imagined.

When this occurs

1. Respond, Don't react! If these situations trigger you to lose your temper, breathe. Take three deep breaths and ask yourself, "do I feel any better?" If not, take three more to make sure you are inhaling deeply, and while you're exhaling, you're releasing all the air in your lungs completely. You will have moments when you want to break out in a temper tantrum like a 2-year-old kicking and screaming on the floor, but let's face it, that's not going to help anybody. So keep your head high and your temper intact and take ten deep breaths.
2. Stop comparing yourself to her. Stepparenting isn't a race or a competition. We are all here for the kids, so

let's focus on that. You're going to have days when your stepkids act up or try to test you. Just know all kids act up to their parents sometimes.

3. If you choose to be a bonus mom and add value to your stepchild's life, your SC will have words of praise for you one day. It might not come until they're well into their adult life. Some of the best advice I have heard from fellow mom-blogger Jamie Scrimgeour was always remembering what you want your stepchildren to remember. Do you want them to remember the fighting and arguing, or want them to have joyful memories? I'm betting since you're reading this, you want the latter of the two.

Affirmation:

1. My role isn't to replace your mother; it adds love and value to your life. I'll always treat you with love and respect.
2. You can't control how someone else acts. You can control how you react to it.

Journal Prompt: Stressors

- What are my top two stressors in my stepmom role? How can I think about these two things differently?
- You get to choose how you want to feel and handle your stepmom stressors. Write out how you want your role as a stepmom to feel. What are three steps you can take to deal with and reduce your stressors?

CHAPTER 2

STEP 2 - BOUNDARIES

"BOUNDARIES - A LINE THAT MARKS THE LIMITS OF A RELATIONSHIP"

- D. STEWART

What is a boundary? It is an invisible line between you and others that allows you to decide what type of access from others you'll allow. Sometimes your boundaries will be tight- you want to love them from afar. Sometimes you'll forget how to set the boundaries, maybe around your kids or spouse. The point is, you make them, and you get to decide if, when, and how you'll adjust them.

How do you create a boundary? You decide what you'll allow from a relationship and whether or not the other party respects that determines your boundary. An excellent example of this is when his high conflict ex makes you feel inadequate by always putting you down in front of the kids or telling your stepkids they don't have to listen to you. Now you are grown, you can decline a relationship with that person (you get to teach them how to treat you) - that's a boundary. Or maybe you limit their access to you - this is also a boundary. Regardless of which you choose, you get to choose. It's okay to have friends and family members that you love a lot but won't spend lots of time with them. Maybe you can only bear to call your family once a month. That is a boundary, and they are healthy. Boundaries get a bad rap because people perceive them to be mean or rude, but they are precisely the opposite. A boundary allows you to have safe and healthy interactions with others. You always get to choose where to set the boundary, which will often change throughout your interactions with others.

Examples of stepmom boundaries

- Time - Making time for yourself or stepping away when you need a minute to process or decide how to respond
- Responsibilities with your partner- Who does what are you going to discipline your stepkids? What our house rules, and how are we going to enforce them.
- Schedules and chauffeuring - Who is responsible for school pickup and dropoff. Who will make plans and coordinate the plans for family events?
- Finances - How will we structure our finances and accounts and our household budget.

Enforcing your Boundaries is an important step in having healthy boundaries. If you don't enforce them, they won't work. So decide what your boundaries are and develop ways to enforce them in different scenarios, so you are prepared.

We teach people how to treat us. If we allow them to be disrespectful, then that is what we will get. It isn't always easy. However, some things aren't negotiable. We must enforce them for the people around us to learn how to interact with us. Some relationships can be harder to do this with than others, but in time and practice, you'll get it.

5 WAYS TO SET HEALTHY BOUNDARIES

Communicate What You Need

Tell the people around you what you need and how you are feeling. When you communicating what you need the people around you to give them an opportunity to give you what you need.

To Reflect Inner Values

Are you being you? Honor your feelings and values in your daily actions and relationships

Know What Works for You

Take care of you first! You are the only one that knows what works for you and how to take care of yourself first. Remember you can't pour from an empty cup.

Reinforce Your Need

Reinforce your needs with matching behavior. Do what you say you're going to do. Treat yourself the way you want to be treated.

Feel Balanced

Feel balanced and proud of yourself for enforcing your boundaries. This allows you to feel more peaceful and balanced.

@thebonusmommyofficial
Learn more at thebonusmommy.com

Affirmation:

Boundaries and rules put in place to protect my mental health and my energy. It is up to me to teach others where my boundaries are.

Journal Prompt:

- Stressors What are my top two stressors in my stepmom role? How can I think about these two things differently?
- What are three steps you can take to deal with and reduce your stressors?
- You get to choose how you want to feel and handle your stepmom stressors. Write out how you want your role as a stepmom to feel. List three things you want to feel in your stepmom role.

CHAPTER 3

STEP - 3 ASK FOR HELP

"THE FIRST STEP TO FINDING PEACE IS TO REALIZE WHAT YOU CAN AND CAN'T CONTROL." - D. STEWART

Alright, you made it this far. Congratulations! You're my people! I'm so proud of you for taking the time to invest in yourself and your bonus mom role and to reach out and get help. You are crushing it!

Sometimes, we do all the journaling, meditating, googling, and letting go that we can, and we still feel like trash. We feel defeated and unable to keep up. I'm here to tell you it's okay to ask for help. We don't discuss and normalize mental health enough in our society, so I'm here to say to you: Therapy is Cool! We need therapy and think we don't (hello, denial!). You must have the tools you need to be prosperous and healthy, and we can't always do it on our own.

How to find a therapist -

The first step to getting started with therapy is to invest some time in finding someone that YOU feel comfortable around. I recommend you interview potential therapists. If you start working with someone but don't feel like you click, it's ok to look for someone else. If you don't, you won't share, defeating the purpose.

If you have insurance, call your insurance carrier and check to see your mental health benefits. Ask if they're therapists in your area that your insurance recommends or what offices are in-network with your insurance. You want to know what is covered (do you have a copay, deductible, etc.).

Take your time to make sure you like the person. You aren't going to address what's going on in your head in one session.

Asking your therapist how often they recommend you come in and schedule a recurring time slot on their calendar. That way, you can't make excuses for not going. No, girl, you are doing this.

Suppose you didn't feel good about your introductory appointment, schedule one with someone else. Maybe in the same office or find someone new. I use Google and Facebook reviews. You can also go to your state board site and see who is in your area.

Asking for help in other areas.

As a stepmom, you wear many hats, cook, housekeeper, teacher/tutor, wife, etc. It's ok to admit that you need help. Let others support you in your life in areas you don't enjoy so you can focus on the tasks you're good at doing.

Do you have a girlfriend who might need a break from her kids? Then arrange to do kid swaps, and she takes your kids for a few hours one day, and you do the same another day. It serves two purposes: you both get time away to do the things you need to do or to take a break and have time by yourself.

Maybe you don't like to cook or do it so much that you might be sick if you cook one more dish. Ask your husband for help. Or come up with super easy things to make that the kids can help you. It might not seem like much, but just that help one day out of the week will help.

Asking for help isn't always the easiest thing to do, but it's ok to ask. Because we need help, we can't do everything by ourselves, nor do we want to.

Find Support -

If you have friends or family members that aren't step-parents or don't have to deal with a high-conflict ex, then there's a good chance they might not understand what it's like to be in your position, and that's okay. No, you're not out of your mind. You need to find people that can relate to you and are in similar situations. It doesn't mean your friends and family don't love you or don't want to support you; they might not understand how to go about it. In my experience, some people figured it out after they saw me in my role as a stepmom; others still didn't get it. Despite that, I did and am still doing what I do. The best tip for you is to reach out and find support and help. It can be a support group, bonus moms group online, or a therapist.

Support Who will understand better than you what you're going through on your bonus mom journey than a fellow bonus mom? You need support. You aren't alone and don't have to feel alone. Lean on others and allow them to help. There will be times when you lean on others for support, and it isn't working like it once did. You may need more help than just a fellow friendly ear. Do NOT hold back. Ask for help before it gets out of hand. Take it from me, I did a couple of years of clinical therapy on top of the self-care and releasing techniques I did for years before then.

There were times when I thought, "will this ever get better?" There can be dark times when you're so frustrated because you can't fix your spouse and stepchild relationships. Having an absent parent is painful to watch someone go through, just like watching your spouse deal with a high conflict EX.

Affirmation:

I am whole, and I am perfect just the way I am! I am learning and growing! I set the tone and the vibe for my whole family.

Journal Prompt:

List 15 things that you love about yourself. Anytime you start to doubt yourself, look at this list and remember you are perfect just the way you are

CHAPTER 4

STEP 4 - SELF CARE

"SELF-CARE IS HOW YOU TAKE YOUR POWER BACK" - LALAH DELIA

What is self-care, you ask? It's the act of caring for yourself and your needs first. You can't do self-care unless you're just not doing it. The most crucial thing to remember is to take CARE of YOURSELF. It can look different for all of us and can be as simple as sitting down to drink your coffee for 5 minutes in the morning.

I want to give you everything you need to take care of yourself, so here are my favorite self-care activities.

5 Best Self Care Activities

Task: Self Care

Goal: Take the time to nurture yourself

1. Take a bath or a hot shower. During my baths, I en-

vision myself floating effortlessly, just existing. Maybe you don't have time to take a bath. You can do this during your shower. Put your head under the shower and envision the water washing away all your worries. They are slowly leaving your body running down the drain. You can also add your favorite essential oil, bath salts, or bath bombs.
2. Yoga and meditation. Make it simple! You can find fabulous free short meditations on YouTube or search on your favorite podcast APP. You'll feel so much better if you move your body and clear your head, even if it's only for 5-10 minutes.
3. Drink your morning coffee warm or make a mocktail in the afternoon.
4. Go for a walk. Tie up your sneakers and start walking! Just a few minutes can ultimately make a difference. Invest in yourself. Buy yourself something you've been wanting: a cute sweater, training to learn a new skill, a gym membership, or that yoga class you've wanted to take. It doesn't have to be expensive or extravagant, just in something that benefits you. You'll be amazed at how much it'll help the people around you too.
5. Take the time to care for yourself. When mom is taken care of, so is everyone else!

Affirmation:

I am worthy and deserving of everything I desire. If it is my desire, it is for me.

Journal Prompt:

What is troubling you?

Why are you upset about it? Write it all out... Let the words come out on the page like vomit (gross I know, but I just want you to write it down). It doesn't have to be perfect. You just have to get it out. I promise you, sis, you will feel amazing! Feel better? Great,

Now it's time to clean up your side of the street.

Write out what you can do and ways you can clean up that vomit. Is there a situation you faulted in?

Go apologies. Are there things that you are overreacting to? Let it go because you deserve to be happy.

CHAPTER 5

STEP 5- CONFIDENCE

"DO WHAT YOU FEEL IN YOUR HEART TO BE RIGHT- FOR YOU'LL BE JUDGED ANYWAY. YOU'LL BE DAMNED IF YOU DO, AND DAMNED IF YOU DON'T." - ELEANOR ROOSEVELT

Do your best and forget the rest.

At the beginning of my bonus mom journey, I was stressed. I was worried I would mess it up or say something wrong, but once I started to get into it and see the bigger picture, I gained insight into the best way to go about it. The biggest thing I can do is tell you to do the best you can in every situation and then forget the rest. Sometimes crappy things happen, and sometimes relationships are just hard. You are enough; you are worthy. You are doing it right, so forget the rest! Throw that trash out the window.

Be so focused on you and who you are so when someone comes to judge you or not understand your situation it's ok.

It doesn't bother you because you're so focused on your side of the street and the things you can control you don't notice what is happening on the other side of the street. This is not to say you are conceited or living in a fantasy land what it means is that you are working on focusing on your crap, your drama, the things you can control that you aren't worried about anything else.

Affirmation:

I will focus on myself and do me! I will not be worried about what others think because I know my intentions are good.

Journaling prompts:

List five things you do well. These five things come naturally to you, and your friends and family often come to you for advice or help in these areas.

Now list two things you want to be better at or things you want to do better. Now take those two things and come up with three steps for each of your weaknesses and list steps you can take to improve in these areas.

Desiree Stewart is an entrepreneur, wife, mom, and stepmom who started her stepmom journey 15 years ago. She has faced challenges and adversities in her stepmom role and wants to help other stepmoms thrive and be happier in their role. When she isn't writing, or building her businesses she is with her family and their three dogs enjoying the Pacific Northwest.

www.ingramcontent.com/pod-product-compliance
Lightning Source LLC
Chambersburg PA
CBHW071418290426
44108CB00014B/1875